PURPOSE
UNLEASHED

EDWRIN V.B. SUTTON

DEDICATION

This book is dedicated to everyone that has had a dream, a desire to make the world better, been rejected, been abandoned and has felt lost in life. This book is for you and to you. There is purpose on your life.

CONTENTS

PREFACE

I've learned to not allow ones facts to become ones truth. Facts are tangible statistics. Truth is a tangible or an intangible absolute. Facts may change. Truth is immutable. Facts are based on knowledge, while truth is based on knowing. Knowledge bears witness to information. However, knowing bears witness to conviction.

It is a fact that as a child I was clinically labeled as mildly autistic. It is a fact that I scored the highest that a student could score on both Math and English exams while in the seventh grade, yet flunked the seventh grade with a 69 in Math for the year. It is a fact that I was voted Class President my freshmen year of High School but then dropped out of school my senior year. It is a fact that I was a serial-monogamist which gave the illusion to others that I was a womanizing polygamist. It is a fact that I used profanity, smoked "weed" and for a season was flirting with the street life. These are the facts, but none of these were, nor is the truth.

What I am is not the same as "Who I am". What I am is my description, but who I am is my definition. Although many saw what I was, the flunky, the mildly autistic and so forth, it did not stop me from becoming who I am, "The child of God." My facts didn't stop me from becoming God's truth!

I remember dating while in High School. Although at the time the facts were that I was unemployed and not known prominently outside of but a couple of counties, I recall telling young ladies in whom I was dating whenever I felt they treated me with a level of disrespect, a truth that reflected an inward conviction. I would say to them, "You better be careful how you treat me because you are going to see me on TV one day. You will read about me one day and you will be sorry for how you treated me." Lo and behold, I've appeared on National Christian television several times. For being productive in my profession I've been deemed as "news worthy", by the grace of God. I've shared the stage with some of the greatest Gospel Artists of this generation and I've shared the platform with some of the most influential preachers of the western part of the world. I am also known by some notable personalities, both sacred and secular. I've played leading roles in several off-Broadway productions and was also featured in two films. I always had a conviction of this truth, that I would be a prominent figure. However, I thought I was going to be an entertainer. Who would have ever thought that I would be a Preacher of the Gospel? However, this convicting truth trumped my convincing facts. Today, I am a happily married man, a Pastor and a man of discipline and principle, all because purpose was unleashed.

I wrote this book out of deep compassion for others and out of a burdensome conviction from God. I noticed many individuals not having a clue as to what they were put on this Earth to do. Seeing loved ones, church associates, family and even celebrities wasting their life deeply disturbed me. As God placed the idea of this book in my spirit, with the subsequent prompting, He then sent people within the span of 30 days to confirm that the writing of this book was the will of God. I say this cautiously and humbly, but yet boldly. God has given me a strong sense of purpose. Some might say, "What can a 30-year-old tell me about purpose?" Well, the Late Dr. Martin Luther King Jr. while in his 30's demonstrated a unique sensitivity of purpose that I am sure we can all learn from. Moreover, Jesus Christ of Nazareth began to walk in the purpose of His ministry when He was 30 years of age. Respectfully and sensibly, I dare not claim to be either of the two. What I would like to claim is that wisdom does not come with age. Wisdom comes with stage. Just because you grew old doesn't mean that you grew up.

It is my hope that as the Lord has shared with me, you will allow me to share with you. This book has been unleashed so that your purpose will be unleashed!

ACKNOWLEDGMENTS

I gladly acknowledge my wife, Nakia, my right hand in every aspect of my life. You are my lover, you've become my best friend, my business partner and most importantly you're my sister in Christ. You make life taste better. I am very excited to see that you are walking in your purpose. I am proud of you! Stay the course and watch God help you finish the race.

I am very grateful for and to my mother and father, Dr. Valentine Sutton and the late Edward Sutton Sr. As grandparents, you adopted me as your own and prepared me for my purpose. I thank God for you. Without God using you, I would not be where it is that I am today.

To my father Ben, sister Shannon, and brothers Antione and Terrance, I thank God that the Lord has placed each one of you in my heart and life.

To the AME Zion Church, thank you for utilizing my gifts and experiences. I am honored to be a part of such an impactful and historic extension of The Kingdom of God.

To my Bishop, The Right Reverend Dennis V. Proctor, thank you for your correction and encouragement. I value you as my leader and as a "Man of God."

To my mentor, Bishop Michael A. Blue, thank you for your profound wisdom, insight and leadership. You have been a breath of fresh air in this new season of my life. I am learning and growing by sitting under your teachings.

To my father in the ministry, Pastor George W. Maize IV, thank you for contributing to a major level of my foundation. Although you are no longer my Pastor, you will forever be my father in the ministry. I am that I am because of God's grace and your discipline.

INTRODUCTION

*In the beginning God created the heaven and the earth. And the earth
was without form, and void; and darkness was upon the face of the
deep. And the Spirit of God moved upon the face of the waters.*
— GENESIS 1:1-2 KJV

We discover and may adequately identify these words as the preface of Scripture. Here in the beginning of Genesis, we find God introducing three essentials. Essential #1, God introduces Himself; Essential #2, God introduces Scripture; and Essential #3, God introduces the pre-creational state of the Earth.

It is worth noting that God introduces the Earth with three distinct aspects. First, it is "without form," *having no definite shape*. Secondly, it is "void," *empty or not satisfied*, and thirdly, it is overtaken by "darkness," *having no light or direction*. We see a perfect description of what it looks like when something or someone is not walking in purpose.

Without Form

An individual who is either unaware of his or her purpose, or simply is not walking therein, is "without form." These individuals are absent of any definite shape. You cannot ever identify them as being a square, a triangle or any other shape for that matter. They are always going back and forth, back and forth. They are double-minded, inconsistent, and often unstable. One day they are extremely joyful and the next day they are extremely sorrowful. They never seem to grasp a constant emotion, ambition, or sometimes even lifestyle.

Perhaps you are the one described. Are you constantly changing career ambitions, from nurse to actor to school teacher? Have you changed your college major more than twice? Do you often change the city wherein you reside? Maybe you just go from one extreme to the next in regard to a relationship preference, jumping from "gangster" to "gentleman," much older to much younger, or different sex to same sex. If you found yourself in any of these categories, you are indeed "without form."

It is very challenging for others to identify who you are if in fact, you cannot identify who you are. For this reason, many of us live our lives reaching for people subconsciously hoping that they will give our lives meaning and definition. We seek relationships believing that the person in whom we are anticipating a relationship with will make us feel better about who we are. However, the only one that can truly identify you and correctly define you is God, your Creator. Whenever you willingly omit purpose, God still defines you but His identification of you on the Earth alters.

It is very challenging for others to identify who you are if, in fact, you cannot identify who you are.

> *And the LORD God called unto Adam, and said unto him, Where art thou?* — GENESIS 3:9 KJV

After Adam and Eve willfully disobeyed God and willfully omitted purpose, God asked Adam, the one in whom He gave domestic leadership responsibility to, "Where art thou?" Our Creator did not ask Adam this question because He did not know where Adam was. God is omniscience, all knowing. He knew exactly where Adam was, but He wanted Adam to know that although God still defined Adam as "His," He no longer identifies with or relates to Adam in the same manner. The word *Adam* in the Hebrew text means *man*. God is simply asking, "What happened to mankind? Adam, do you realize you lost your place? Adam, do you realize that we will no longer converse as friend to friend, but you will soon have to call on my name?" For many of you reading, God is asking you this same question. What has happened to you? Is this the life that I intended for you? Is this who I created you to be before the foundation of the world? I believe that as you continue to read this book, God is going to give you the "form" that you have been so desperately desiring.

Void

The term "void" means "to be empty." It also denotes one being unfulfilled or unsatisfied. Individuals who do not walk in their purposes are often very miserable. They do not want to get out of bed. They do not enjoy going to the place of their employment. They awaken on Monday only to dream about the close of Friday. The spouse never wants to come home to his or her family. The teenager never leaves his or her room. The pastor dreads mounting the pulpit on Sunday morning. And, the teacher is sickened of the thought of a classroom. These individuals are void of purpose. They exist, but still do not have life. Existence says, "I am here." Life says, "I am glad I am here." Existence says, "I am here." Life says, "I know why I am here." Those who are not walking in purpose feel mummified and not mobilized; zombies just going through the motions without having the adequate emotions. Do you ever feel as if you are a cast member of "The Walking Dead?"

The absence of purpose, to a certain magnitude, is the common denominator found in polygamists, serial-monogamists, pornography addicts, gossip pundits, drug and alcohol abusers, and all others who are living contrary to God's plan for their lives. To some degree, they are either deprived of realized (in conscious) purpose or actualized (in practice) purpose. These ungodly and unfulfilling acts are simply outward anesthetics do to an inward antagonism. It is our inward cry for help, satisfaction and purpose that provokes us to abusive, immoral, and chronic behavior. The individuals who are aware of their purposes but are not yet walking therein, are often faced with such "demons". Just think about it. If you know your purpose but are not walking in your purpose, you are probably bored, lazy and unproductive. This is the breeding ground for many, if not all, unhealthy addictions. What is it that the saints of old would say? "An idle mind is the Devil's workshop." This, my friends, has proven itself to be true.

Darkness

The Earth was dark. Therefore, we can conclude that there was an absence of light. And if there was an absence of light, there was also an absence of direction. The Earth was lost. The Earth did not have any sense of direction. Consequently, the Earth stayed stagnant.

When we do not realize our purposes, direction is foreign. We exist in life without a clue. We seem to go wherever the wind blows, always asking questions, but never seeming to find answers. In this pitiful state of being, we aim for the proverbial piñata blindfolded, always confused, always out of place, out of time, out of "purpose." Because of this darkness, many individuals' theology changes unproductively from season to season to season. And, since they don't have any direction, they conclude that, "Wherever I walk and wherever I end up must be destiny and truth, since it is my reality."

Does this sound like you? Have you been trying to figure out what to do with your life? Since you do not know which way to go, have you become stuck, stagnate and still? Do you suffer from "option paralysis;" having so many choices and options that it overwhelms you to the degree that you do not choose anything at all? Have the majority of the choices you've made produced negative results? Are you afraid to make your own choices? Do you see your past in color, but your future in black and white? If so my friend, you are living in a measure of darkness because of the lack of purpose.

There is Hope

Although the Earth was not "in" purpose, the Earth still "had" purpose. Praise be unto God! You might not be existing in purpose, but you still exist on purpose because you exist for a purpose. Ultimately, even your condition of not being in purpose is still working for your purpose.

You might not be existing in purpose, but you still exist on purpose because you exist for a purpose.

The Holy Scriptures declare:

And we know that all things work together for good to them that love
God, to them who are the called according to his purpose.
— ROMANS 8:28 KJV

If God saw a wasted, inauspicious, unprepossessing Earth and gave it distinction, dilation, and direction, just imagine what it is that the Lord is going to do in you. You may be a mess now, but you're going to be a message later. You may be damaged goods now, but you're going to be a desired need later. There is hope for you young brother. There is hope for you single sister. There is hope for you who have no definite identity. There is hope for you who feel empty inside. There is hope for you who have no direction. Christ came to give hope and purpose to the atheist. Christ came to give hope and purpose to the black supremacist. Christ came to give hope and purpose to the white supremacist. Christ came to give hope and purpose to the individual who is struggling with his or her sexuality. Christ came to give hope and purpose to that young man who has been abandoned by his father. Christ came to give hope and purpose to the prostitute and stripper. Christ came to give hope and purpose to all: the lost, the left-out, and the left-overs.

As you read this book and receive the love of Jesus the Christ in a greater more conscious way, God is going to unleash purpose to you. Eyes have not seen, nor have ears heard, neither has it entered into the heart of man, the things that God has prepared for you if you love Him! If you believe it and are willing to correctly respond to it say, "Amen!"

Chapter 1
THE PURPOSE OF PURPOSE

Have you ever taken the time to think on what is the purpose of purpose? I know that sounds a little unusual, but think about it. Why would God give mankind a purpose collectively and individually? Why couldn't we just exist for existence sake? Why couldn't we have been created to do whatever we wanted to do? Doesn't this seem less burdensome and more carefree? How undemanding this would be to wake-up every morning whenever we like, to do whatsoever we choose. I mean, wouldn't we love and appreciate God more? These questions are very thought provoking. But for every question there is an answer.

When you ask the question, "What is the purpose of my purpose?" you are really asking, "What is the general purpose of my specific purpose?" There are three essential components of the general purpose of the specific purpose of your life. Stated in another way, there are three answers to the question "Why?"

Bless God

One of the reasons for which God gave us all a purpose is because it is impossible to please God or bless God if we are not walking in our purposes. I know what it is that many of you are thinking. "I thought the Scriptures say that without faith it is impossible to please God? It does not say without purpose!" What you are thinking is true. However, what is faith? My father in the ministry, Pastor George Maize IV says that faith is correctly responding to what God said. I totally agree! Simply put, you cannot please God if you do not do what it is that He tells you to do. You cannot please God if you do not become what it is that He made you or told you to become. You cannot please God if you are a police officer, but He created you to be a school teacher. You cannot please God if you are simply serving on the usher board, but He has called you to serve in the pulpit.

It is equivalent to an inventor creating a new product. The idea in the inventor's mind is that there would be a product that instantly freezes food. You simply place the food in the mechanism, set the timer for two or four minutes, depending upon the substance and the quantity of the food item, and instantly it freezes. However, once the creator makes this creation or invention, instead of freezing food it warms up food. The inventor is not pleased for a couple of reasons. First, he or she is not pleased because the creation does not produce what it was supposed to produce. Secondly, the creator is not pleased because he or she has already created the microwave, the stove, and the oven for heating food. Therefore, this product that is not producing what it was created to supply is deemed no good.

> *God has given each of you a gift from his great variety of spiritual gifts. Use them well to serve one another. Do you have the gift of speaking? Then speak as though God himself were speaking through you. Do you have the gift of helping others? Do it with all the strength and energy that God supplies.* **Then everything you do will bring glory to God through Jesus Christ.** *All glory and power to him forever and ever.* — 1 PETER 4:10-11 NLT

This Scripture will serve as one of our theme Scriptures throughout the entirety of this book. As you read this Scripture, the Apostle Peter is simply saying, "Do what you were created to do." But then he informs us that by us doing that which God has called us to do, God is glorified and pleased.

It pleases God when His creation functions in the way and for the purpose that it was created to function. If you want to bless God, (make Him happy) walk in your purpose. Walking by faith in your purpose excites God!

Bless Others

Let us look again at this passage of Scripture:

11

God has given each of you a gift from his great variety of spiritual gifts. **Use them well to serve one another.** *Do you have the gift of speaking? Then speak as though God himself were speaking through you. Do you have the gift of helping others? Do it with all the strength and energy that God supplies. Then everything you do will bring glory to God through Jesus Christ. All glory and power to him forever and ever.* — 1 PETER 4:10-11 NLT

The purpose of your purpose is to bless others. If you do not have a conscious awareness that you are blessing others, you are not walking in the fullness of your purpose. This Scripture tells us to use our gifts well, to serve one another. If you are a millionaire but are not using your resources and influence to bless others, you are not walking in the fullness of your purpose. If you are a celebrity or a celebrity type, but are not using your resources and influence to bless others, you are not walking in the fullness of your purpose.

If you do not have a conscious awareness that you are blessing others, you are not walking in the fullness of your purpose.

It is so fulfilling and rewarding when you know that God has used you to make a persons' life better. There is a prominent sense of peace and purpose when you have richly blessed someone. That is how God intended it to be. Mankind was created to bless God, but mankind was also created to bless mankind.

Each and every one of us has a special gift or gifts from the LORD that we are supposed to use to serve mankind. How are you contributing to the welfare of society? Are you a great gift and giver to the world? Are persons' lives bettered because of you? Is your place of employment blessed because you are there? Can people say that if it had not been for you and your service things would be worse off? Or maybe you are one just wasting air; existing only to die.

And he said unto them, Go ye into all the world, and preach the gospel to every creature. — MARK 16:15 KJV

And God blessed them, and God said unto them, Be fruitful, and multiply, and replenish the earth, and subdue it: and have dominion over the fish of the sea, and over the fowl of the air, and over every living thing that moveth upon the earth. — GENESIS 1:28 KJV

In the Gospel according to Mark, Jesus Christ has just been resurrected from the dead and He appears to the 11 Apostles (Judas killed himself so at this time there were only 11 Apostles.). He says to them "*Go ye into all the world, and preach the gospel to every creature.*" Christians know this as "The Great Commission." Let us look at this text a little closer.

Christ says, "Go ye." Ye means, in my southern vernacular "All of ya'll." Christ says that the assignment to go is for all of God's children. But where do we go? He says go into all the world. May I submit to you that Christ is not telling them and us essentially to go into all the Earth. Yes, the Earth is implied here but let's not miss the "BIG PICTURE." Christ says go into all the world, not Earth. These two terms are akin, but they are not synonymous.

The term *world* in the Greek is *kosmos*. In this text, this word means "order, arrangement" or, my favorite application, "system." The Earth is the planet, but the world is the arrangement of systems on the planet. And Christ was intentional when He said go into ALL THE SYSTEM(s). Christ wants individuals to go into the educational systems of the Earth so that we may serve the people and improve the system. Christ wants individuals to go into the political systems of the Earth so that we may serve the people and improve the system. Christ wants individuals to go into the arts and entertainment systems of the Earth so that we may serve the people and improve the system. This is our purpose collectively, but we must find the system that we are called to serve in individually. Yes, it is bigger than the local church assembly!

Although we call this "The Great Commission," Genesis 1:28 was the initial "Great Commission." God tells Adam and Eve five necessities; be fruitful, multiply, replenish, subdue and dominate. However, I want to only tackle the first three.

When we read this Scripture, initially we usually only think with the mindset that God is telling Adam and Eve to have a lot of children. Again, this is implied, but this viewpoint does not reveal the meat of the matter. God is saying produce (be fruitful) in abundance (multiply) to the point the Earth is full (replenish the earth). God's intention is that we would make the world better. How can I say that? How can man improve upon that which a perfect God has created?

God's intention is that we would make the world better.

"For the kingdom of heaven is like a man traveling to a far country, who called his own servants and delivered his goods to them. And to one he gave five talents, to another two, and to another one, to each according to his own ability; and immediately he went on a journey. Then he who had received the five talents went and traded with them, and made another five talents. And likewise he who had received two gained two more also. But he who had received one went and dug in the ground, and hid his lord's money. After a long time the lord of those servants came and settled accounts with them.

"So he who had received five talents came and brought five other talents, saying, 'Lord, you delivered to me five talents; look, I have gained five more talents besides them.' His lord said to him, 'Well done, good and faithful servant; you were faithful over a few things, I will make you ruler over many things. Enter into the joy of your lord.' He also who had received two talents came and said, 'Lord, you delivered to me two talents; look, I have gained two more talents besides them.' His lord said to him, 'Well done, good and faithful servant; you have been faithful over a few things, I will make you ruler over many things. Enter into the joy of your lord.'

"Then he who had received the one talent came and said, 'Lord, I knew you to be a hard man, reaping where you have not sown, and gathering where you have not scattered seed. And I was afraid, and went and hid your talent in the ground. Look, there you have what is yours.'

"But his lord answered and said to him, 'You wicked and lazy servant, you knew that I reap where I have not sown, and gather where I have not scattered seed. 27 So you ought to have deposited my money with the bankers, and at my coming I would have received back my own with interest. Therefore take the talent from him, and give it to him who has ten talents.

'For to everyone who has, more will be given, and he will have abundance; but from him who does not have, even what he has will be taken away. And cast the unprofitable servant into the outer darkness. There will be weeping and gnashing of teeth.'

— MATTHEW 25:14-30 KJV

We see in this passage of Scripture that the ruler expected his servants to increase or to improve that which he had entrusted to them. He rewarded those who improved it. He blessed those who increased it. But there was one who didn't increase it, yet he did not worsen it either. The ruler was upset. Wouldn't you think that since what the servant was given didn't depreciate, the Master would have been okay? At least it was in the same condition that the Master initially left it in, right? If you gave me one hundred dollars to hold for you while you went on vacation and when you returned I still had the one hundred dollars wouldn't you be pleased? Well, God does not want what it is that He entrusted to us to be in the same condition when He returns. God expects for us to improve that which He has entrusted us with. To some degree we have! Look around! In the Garden of Eden, there was not any electricity, television, refrigerators, automobiles, internet, Wal-Mart or Verizon Wireless. It was not in the garden, but it was in the man. God has placed ideas, concepts and gifts on the inside of us so that we can bless others and improve the systems of the Earth. Bishop Michael Blue, Pastor of The Door of Hope Christian Church in Marion, SC, gave me this viewpoint. He also says that our purpose is to make a world (system) and to make a world (system) better. We are here to improve what it is that God has entrusted us with. This is why it is a sin for you not to produce the CD when God has put in your spirit original music. God gave you this "music" so that you can enhance it and so that it will enhance others. This is why it is a sin for you to have so much knowledge and wisdom, but you never put it in a book or take the time to mentor someone. God gave you that knowledge so that you can enhance it and so that it will enhance others. God does not approve when what it is He gave us has not improved.

> *A man's gift maketh room for him, and bringeth him before great men.* — PROVERBS 18:16 KJV

Proverbs states that a man's gift will make room for him. This is a verse that is often quoted but often misinterpreted. The word *"gift"* in this text and in the Hebrew text is *"mattân."* This word does not simply mean one's skill or talent. One's skill or talent is referenced by this word in this text, but one's skill or talent is not described by this word in this text. The term *gift* or *mattân* refers to what it is that one person gives to another person. It means giving a gift, blessing others. This leads me to the third purpose of purpose.

Bless Self

God has given each one of us gifts to give away. As it relates to our verse in Proverbs, the reason why many of us have not experienced specific desired opened doors and subsequently been in the presence of influential people is simply because we are not using our gifts to serve. Yes, we are gifted, but our problem is that we are not giving. God's system is that as you bless Him and bless others it will in return bless you. Everything you do or don't do in life has a return. Everything! God's will is that you are blessed by blessing Him and others.

There are three primary ways in which your purpose was created to bless you.

Fulfilment

Purpose was created to fulfill you. What a tormenting and agonizing life it is for a person to live unsatisfied. What it is that you are supposed to enjoy does not bring you any pleasure when you are unfulfilled Water ceases from being a thirst quencher. The love of your life becomes nothing more than a "thorn in the flesh." You consistently eat a large helping of food, but you still remain hungry. Purpose gives your life meaning. Purpose causes you to laugh in a painful situation. Purpose enables you to be bold when you have every tangible reason to be afraid. Purpose is that which keeps the caterpillar in the cocoon until the appointed time. Purpose is that which gave "Blacks" a song in the midst of slavery.

God knows that whenever you are not fulfilled, suicide, murder, anger, bitterness, addiction, nervous breakdown, obesity, disease and pre-mature death are knocking at your door. That is why God is going to fulfill you with Himself and His purpose like never before! Just receive it by faith!

Prosperity

Do you know that money is connected to your purpose? Yes! Your purpose was created to pay you! It is true that the poor will be among us always, but what else is true is that poverty was never the will of God. For the young lady who sees herself changing the fashion industry with her ideas, concepts and creativity, money is connected to that. For the musically inclined child that beats on the pots, pans and tables while singing throughout the day, money is connected to that. For the individual who is concerned for the physical health of others and has the passion for medicine, health and people, money is connected to that. Your wealth is not around you. Your wealth is inside of you. Wealth is not what you earn. Wealth is what you produce!

Wealth is not what you earn. Wealth is what you produce!

You are just one idea away from a financial blessing. You are just one leap of faith away from financial stability. Again, what you need is not necessarily around you, but what you need is already inside of you. Just ask yourself! Did you write that book that's been in your spirit for years yet? What about that business that has been in your mind? What have you done with that? Have you used all of your gifts and talents to the max? Always remember that there is seed already inside of the apple. The apple does not beg for seed. The apple is the birther of seed. You are the apple and the seed of wealth resides within your core.

You are just one idea away from a financial blessing.

Acting upon an idea that was within him to leave West Virginia and move to Dallas, Texas, was the initial determining factor of the success of a poor country preacher whom we know as Bishop TD Jakes. Acting upon an idea to create a network for students for one university was the initial determining factor of the success of the billionaire and Facebook founder, in whom we all appreciate, Mark Zuckerberg. Acting upon an idea to do stage-plays all across the world, despite a series of poorly attended shows while even being homeless for a season, was the initial determining factor for the millionaire success that we know as Tyler Perry. Financial prosperity is attached to your God-given purpose if you act upon the right idea.

The truth is that you may never be rich in finances like these individuals, but when you walk in your purpose a level of finance follows you. This is true! However, if your reasoning for doing something is simply based on how much money you will receive, then it is not the plan of God for your life. It is only when you seek to bless God by blessing others that your service will in return bless you.

> *Therefore take no thought, saying, What shall we eat? or, What shall we drink? or, Wherewithal shall we be clothed? (For after all these things do the Gentiles seek:) for your heavenly Father knoweth that ye have need of all these things. But seek ye first the kingdom of God, and his righteousness; and all these things shall be added unto you.*
> —MATTHEW 6:31-33 KJV

Life Insurance

My friends! Whenever you are walking in your purpose in Christ Jesus, you have life insurance. Your life is protected when you are walking in purpose. You cannot die until you are ready to die when you are walking in purpose!

> *I have fought a good fight, I have finished my course, I have kept the faith:* — 2 TIMOTHY 4:7 KJV

> *When Jesus therefore had received the vinegar, he said, It is finished: and he bowed his head, and gave up the ghost.*
> — JOHN 19:30 KJV

In November of the year 2014, Dr. Myles Munroe, one of the greatest articulators of the Christian faith of our time, died by way of a plane accident. In one of his last media interviews which was held on October of 2014, Dr. Monroe stated that there was nothing left and that he was ready to die. Then the following month he died. He knew his assignment was complete.

You cannot die until you are ready to die when you are walking in purpose.

The Apostle Paul declared that because he had finished his purpose and his assignment on the Earth that it was his time to die. Then he died. Jesus Christ, while on the cross said, "It is finished." Then He died.

Oh what a blessed hope! God has ordained it so that as we are doing His will and fulfilling our purpose on the Earth, death cannot touch us until we are finished with our assignment. You cannot die prematurely if you are living purposefully. If you are walking in purpose you have the legal right to tell sickness, in Jesus' Name, to get off of you because it is not your time to die. When you are walking in purpose, you have the legal right to tell death, in Jesus' Name, to stand still because your work is not done. If you are doing what it is that God has created you to do, then God will not allow you to die until you've finished His assignment for you on the Earth. You ought to take some time now to praise the LORD!

Make a Decision

Before you discover your specific purpose and walk therein, you must first make the conscious decision to surrender to God's general purpose for all of mankind. Make the decision today to bless God. Make the decision today to bless others. And if you have made these two decisions, consequently you have made the decision to bless yourself. Do not allow fear to rob you of your purpose. You have nothing else to lose but your will. It has been your will that has kept you from fulfilling and possibly discovering your purpose. Make the decision to give yourself away. Make the decision to live a new life. Make the decision to live free and fulfilled.

If you are ready to go on this journey pray this prayer out loud:

"Father God, I thank you for creating me, for I realize that you do not make any mistakes and you spoke me in existence and placed me on the Earth for a specific reason. I acknowledge my sin, selfishness and stubbornness and I repent. I make the decision to give my life fully to you through your son Jesus who I believe is the Christ. I am willing to say "Yes" to you even before you tell me that which you would have me to do. Please reveal to me my purpose so that I may bless you, bless others and bless myself. Thank you for seeing greatness in the midst of the mess. In Jesus' Name I pray, Amen."

Chapter 2
UNLEASHED THROUGH PRAYER

So often, we desire yet bypass more lucid revelation because we omit God's simple applications. Prayer is one of the simplest yet most profound applications that God has graced mankind with. Prayer is becoming a long lost discipline and resource in our society. Schools are no longer praying. Families are no longer praying. And even local church assemblies are no longer praying.

Prayer is the means in which mankind communicates with Almighty God. Well, some might question the legitimacy of prayer. If God is omniscience, all-knowing, then why should I pray? Bishop Michael Blue, whom I might reference throughout the entirety of this book, says that prayer does not inform God, but prayer invites God. I totally agree! However, I would like to build upon that thought. Prayer does not inform God, but prayer invites God to inform mankind. When you speak to God, God will speak to you and you will hear Him.

> *Trust in the LORD with all thine heart; and lean not unto thine own understanding. In all thy ways acknowledge him, and he shall direct thy paths.* —PROVERBS 3:5-6 KJV

There are many aspects or variables in regards to acknowledging God. However, one of the most practical and fundamental means of acknowledging God is through prayer. How can one receive direction from a source when one has never sought or asked for direction from the source? God will give you direction in every aspect of your life if you would simply ask for it.

So often have we forfeited direction and clarity in our lives because we have not prayed. What pain would you have circumvented if you would have only applied prayer? Think about it! Would you have bypassed some of the heartbreaks of disillusioned and unfulfilled relationships? Would you have agreed upon certain business deals? Would you have made some of the same educational and career choices?

Prayer is vital to an individual's peace and revelation of purpose.

God will give you direction in every aspect of your life if you simply ask for it.

> *Now there were in the church that was at Antioch certain prophets and teachers; as Barnabas, and Simeon that was called Niger, and Lucius of Cyrene, and Manaen, which had been brought up with Herod the tetrarch, and Saul.*
>
> *As they ministered to the Lord, and fasted, the Holy Ghost said, Separate me Barnabas and Saul for the work whereunto I have called them.* — ACTS 13:1-2 KJV

Here we find an instance in Scripture where purpose is unleashed through prayer. Different individuals were gathered together in Antioch. The Scriptures inform us that as they were gathered they ministered to the LORD. Well, how do you minister to the LORD? For the sake of understanding, there are three categories of ministry that all acts of ministry fall under.

1) **Ministry to the Church** (*Target audience are those who are saved*)
   a) Church Conferences
   b) Bible Studies
   c) Songs like "Victory is Mine"

2) **Ministry to the unchurched** (*Target audience are those who are unsaved*)
   a) Outreach Services (Back 2 School Bash, Tent Revivals Etc.)
   b) Door- to- Door Evangelism
   c) Songs like "God in Me" by Mary Mary & "Stomp" by Kirk Franklin

3) **Ministry to the LORD** (*Target audience is the Creator of both the saved and unsaved*)
   a) Praise & Worship
   b) Prayers of Thanksgiving
   c) Songs like "Holy, Holy, Holy" by John B. Dykes and Reginald Herber & "You Are Good" by Israel & New Breed.

These men of God were ministering to the Lord because they were giving God praise and praying prayers of thanksgiving. Moreover, we know that they were praying because the Scriptures tell us that they were fasting. Fasting as a spiritual discipline is always accompanied with prayer. Fasting is not a substitute for prayer, but it is a complement to prayer. These individuals were wholeheartedly engaging God through praise, possibly psalms and prayer. As they prayed, God, through the Holy Spirit, unleashed purpose.

God revealed to them the "what" of Barnabas and Saul's purpose, the "when" of Barnabas and Saul's purpose, and the "where" of Barnabas and Saul's purpose. Imagine how history would have been edited if these individuals would not have prayed. Since Paul/Saul wrote most of the New Testament Scriptures, if he would have not prayed and purpose had not been unleashed, we would not have the New Testament Scriptures as we know it today. Isn't that powerful? One segment of prayer can alter the entire order of society. Wow!

If you want more clarity in regards to your purpose on the Earth, engage God consistently in prayer. He will reveal to you the what, the when, the where and the how. Speak to Him and He will speak to you.

One segment of prayer can alter the entire order of society.

Come near to God and he will come near to you.
— JAMES 4:8a NIV

Chapter 3
UNLEASHED THROUGH SCRIPTURE

All Scripture is given by inspiration of God, and is profitable for doctrine, for reproof, for correction, for instruction in righteousness, that the man of God may be complete, thoroughly equipped for every good work. — TIMOTHY 3:16-17 KJV

Reading the Word of God is one of the most exciting ways to discover purpose. Everything profitable for purpose sake can be found in Scripture. Therein you will find athletics, war, love, business, fashion, the arts, the medical field, the political system, the judicial system, the educational system, media and so forth. It's all in the Word of God.

Scripture was given by God so that His people would be equipped for every good work. There isn't any aspect of God-given work or purpose that the Word of God doesn't equip you for. In regards to purpose, fundamentally, the Word of God is three-dimensional.

The Three Edged Sword (Penetrator)

For the word of God is quick, and powerful, and sharper than any two edged sword, piercing even to the dividing asunder of soul and spirit, and of the joints and marrow, and is a discerner of the thoughts and intents of the heart. — HEBREWS 4:12 KJV

We often say that the Word of God is a two edged sword. However, the Word of God never says that. What it is that the Scriptures do declare is that the Word of God is sharper than any two-edged sword. In fact, the Word of God has three edges. I like to call the Word of God "The

Three-Edged Sword."

We must remember that mankind was made in God's image and after His likeness. God is triune: God the Father, God the Son, and God the Holy Spirit. Mankind is tripartite, meaning we are made of three parts: spirit, soul, and body, in that order. Often times many individuals believe that mankind is only body and soul, but when they receive Christ they have body, soul, and Holy Spirit. This is not totally true. Although, individuals receive God's Holy Spirit once they believe on Him, confess their sins, and repent, they've still always had a spirit. No, not the Holy Spirit, but the human spirit. Furthermore, to be completely accurate, a human does not truly have a spirit; a human is a spirit that has a soul and body. The real you is spirit. Your essence is spirit. How about this oxymoron? When you die you, do not die. Your body is dead, but you are still living in another realm. Your body is the house that you, the human spirit, lives in. It is the human spirit that houses the Holy Spirit when one becomes a Believer.

We often time confuse the soul with the spirit. Your soul is where your emotions, intellect, creativity, memory and will is housed. These are the aspects of your soul. Your soul enables you to communicate with self. Your spirit enables you to communicate with God. Your body enables you to communicate with others. Some might ask the question, "If your human spirit enables you to communicate with God, then what would be the purpose of the Holy Spirit?" Well, before one has received salvation, he or she can still pray to God. Moreover, before an individual has received salvation, God can even speak to them, especially through dreams. If you study the Scriptures, you will find that God spoke to man and man spoke to God on numerous occasions even though these individuals didn't have the Holy Spirit.

Examples of God speaking to individuals without the Holy Spirit:

- God spoke to Pharaoh through a dream (Genesis 41:1-7)
- God spoke to Moses through the burning bush (Exodus 3:2-22)
- God spoke to Samuel while he was lying down (1 Samuel 3:2-15)
- God spoke to the magi through dreams (Matthew 2:12)

- God spoke to Joseph, Jesus' adopted earthly father, through a dream (Matthew 2:13)
- God spoke to Pilate's wife through a dream (Matthew 27:19)
- God spoke to Saul before he was Paul (Acts 9:3-6)

Examples of individuals praying to God and God granting their request without the Holy Spirit:

- Eliezer prays for God to give Isaac a bride (Genesis 24:12-14)
- Hannah prayed for a son (1 Samuel 1:1-23)
- The sailors prayed for mercy (Jonah 1:11-16)

These are just a few of the many examples of how mankind and God both communicate even without the person having the Holy Spirit. The Holy Spirit intensifies the human spirit. With the Holy Spirit you hear God more clearly, you communicate to God more effectively, and you operate on the Earth for God more powerfully. It is my desire to teach on this more appropriately and convincingly, but maybe this subject will be relinquished until and for another time.

Our author in the book of Hebrews is saying that God's Word is so sharp that it penetrates through the body (bones and marrow), it penetrates through the soul (emotions, will, intellect), and it also strategically and discernably divides the soul from the spirit, not allowing them to hide amongst themselves, dealing with each one intentionally, separately and surgically, penetrating the spirit (the real you). He also describes it as being a discerner of the thoughts and intents of the heart. This is not an added work of the Word, but rather this is our author describing the soulish aspect of the working of the Word. Heart in this context is referring to the inner man: the soul. Not the inner most man: the spirit.

The Word of God penetrates through all of your being. It penetrates through your body (the outer court), your soul (the holy place), and your spirit (the holy of holies). The Word penetrates through your body (your physiology), your soul (your psychology), and your spirit (your pneumatology). With your body the Word purifies you. With your soul the Word rectifies you. With your spirit the Word edifies you. By the

Word, He will deliver your body. By the Word, He is delivering your soul. By the Word, He has delivered your spirit. In other words, with the Word, God will glorify your body. With the Word, God is sanctifying your soul. With the Word, God has salvaged your spirit. The Three Edged Sword of God is a penetrator. This function of the Word of God is very uncomfortable.

The Three-Way Mirror (Examiner)

Do not merely listen to the word, and so deceive yourselves. Do what it says. Anyone who listens to the word but does not do what it says is like someone who looks at his face in a mirror and, after looking at himself, goes away and immediately forgets what he looks like. But whoever looks intently into the perfect law that gives freedom, and continues in it—not forgetting what they have heard, but doing it— they will be blessed in what they do. — JAMES 1:22-25 NIV

The Word of God is also a three-way mirror. The three-edged sword expresses itself as a penetrator, but the three-way mirror expresses itself as a reflector or an examiner. A mirror that has not been manipulated shows you truth. It allows you to see the way you truly appear. It brings you to terms with yourself. A mirror will either affirm you or afflict you. Let me say it in this way. The mirror of the Word of God will comfort you and make you uncomfortable both at the same time. What an encouraging intimidation. The mirror shows you the blemishes. That's uncomfortable. But it allows you to see what it is that needs to be fixed or covered before you engage with the public. That's comforting! I believe that it is safe to say that most all women carry a small mirror in their purse or pocketbook. The mass majority of men do not engage in such "profitable acts." Women hold on to their mirrors for means of both affirmation and correction. If their image meets their standard, then the mirror affirms them. But if to them their image is subpar, the mirror corrects them. Although women and men alike value the mirror for its affirmation and correction, do we value and cling to the "Mirror of the Word" due to the same necessities found therein? Do we only search for the affirming qualities of the Word and disregard it when it corrects that which is not in tact? Do we only apply the makeup that is accompanied with the Mirror of the Word, in which we call grace and mercy, but never apply the cleansing pads that came with the purchase to first wash away our dirt? These are challenging questions that we must ask ourselves. It is God's purpose for our lives that we not only just look better, but that we would also be better.

The mirror of the Word of God will comfort you and make you uncomfortable both at the same time.

A mirror reflects light. It reflects truth. If you do not want truth to be reflected, you should stay out of the mirror. Often times this is the reason why many turn from the Bible. They really do not want light or truth to be reflected. The mirror of the Word reflects light in three fundamental ways.

Reflects Light on Your Past

Have you ever heard the saying, "If you don't know where you've been you won't know where you're going?" In regards to purpose, this is true. The Word of God tells you the truth about your past. It shows you your failures, your mistakes, and your childhood pain. The mirror of the Word wants you to see the truth. The mirror does not want you to live in denial anymore in regards to what it was that happened to you. Yes, they hurt you. Yes, they abandoned you. Yes, you were molested. Yes, you had an abortion. Yes, you cheated on your spouse. Yes, it happened! If you continue to deny your past pain, you will eventually abort your prophetic purpose.

The mirror of the Word also shows you your past successes. It shows your achievements as a child in grade school. It shows you how you were kind, giving, and joyful before you put that soulish wall up. It shows you your success on that project, job, business, or marriage. The mirror shows you the truth about your past successes so you will know that you can continue to succeed.

He that covereth his sins shall not prosper: but whoso confesseth and forsaketh [them] shall have mercy. — PROVERBS 28:13 KJV

If we confess our sins, he is faithful and just to forgive us [our] sins, and to cleanse us from all unrighteousness. — 1 JOHN 1:9 KJV

Then said Jesus to those Jews which believed on him, If ye continue in my word, then are ye my disciples indeed; And ye shall know the truth, and the truth shall make you free. — JOHN 8:31-32 KJV

List the failures of your past that the Word/Jesus Christ is showing you. Be honest with yourself:

1._____

2._____

3._____

4._____

5._____

6._____

7._____

8._____

9._____

10._____

Finally, brothers, whatever is true, whatever is honorable, whatever is just, whatever is pure, whatever is lovely, whatever is commendable, if there is any excellence, if there is anything worthy of praise, think about these things. — PHILIPPIANS 4:8 ESV

The LORD was with Joseph, and he became a successful man, and he was in the house of his Egyptian master. His master saw that the LORD was with him and that the LORD caused all that he did to succeed in his hands. So Joseph found favor in his sight and attended him, and he made him overseer of his house and put him in charge of all that he had. From the time that he made him overseer in his house and over all that he had, the LORD blessed the Egyptian's house for Joseph's sake; the blessing of the LORD was on all that he had, in house and field. So he left all that he had in Joseph's charge, and because of him he had no concern about anything but the food he ate. — GENESIS 39:2-6 ESV

List the successes of your past and the good qualities that you used to have that the Word/Jesus Christ is enabling you to see:

1._____

2._____

3._____

4._____

5._____

6._____

7._____

8._____

9._____

10._____

Reflects Light on Your Present

The mirror shows you the truth in regards to where you are now. It shows you the truth regarding your temper, your lies, your lust, your pride, your laziness, your friendships, your love life, your prayer life, your disobedience, and your sin. It also shows you your productivity, your faith, your maturity, and your strengths. The Word examines you and challenges you to come to terms with what the Word shows you about yourself. A car must be constantly examined for its purpose. Before you serve a meal that you've cooked, it must be examined. Before anyone is allowed to obtain any type of credible license, he or she must first be examined. If we are going to realize purpose and be prepared for purpose, we must allow the mirror of the Word to examine our present state of being for our future destination of becoming.

> *Examine yourselves, to see whether you are in the faith. Test yourselves. Or do you not realize this about yourselves, that Jesus Christ is in you?—unless indeed you fail to meet the test!*
> — 2 CORINTHIANS 13:5 ESV

> *Let a person examine himself, then, and so eat of the bread and drink of the cup. For anyone who eats and drinks without discerning the body eats and drinks judgment on himself. That is why many of you are weak and ill, and some have died. But if we judged ourselves truly, we would not be judged. But when we are judged by the Lord, we are disciplined so that we may not be condemned along with the world.*
> — 1 CORINTHIANS 11:28-32 ESV

> *For by the grace given to me I say to everyone among you not to think of himself more highly than he ought to think, but to think with sober judgment, each according to the measure of faith that God has*

assigned.   — ROMANS 12:3 ESV

Examine your present state through the Word of God. Are you in a good place? Are you in denial about some things? Are you being lazy, productive, mean or loving? Are you still withholding forgiveness in your heart towards someone? Honestly write down the present state of yourself. If you are honest, this can truly bless you:

_____
_____
_____
_____
_____
_____
_____
_____
_____
_____
_____
_____
_____
_____
_____
_____
_____
_____

Reflects Light on Your Future

The Word of God will show you the truth regarding your future. Although, you were raised in an unusual residence, maybe you are purposed to deliver a people like Moses. Yes, as a child you were always left out and your siblings and others seemed to always be the favorites, but maybe you are purposed to sit on the throne like David. You may think that all you have going for yourself is your beauty and grace. But maybe God has purposed you to marry someone of great influence so that you may positively influence their influence like Queen Esther. Or maybe you are a murderer. Maybe you've murdered Christians by your words and actions. Possibly, God has purposed you to be a great soul winner and leader for Him like the Apostle Paul. There is purpose on your life and the mirror of the Word will show you that which it is.

> *For I know the plans I have for you," says the LORD. "They are plans for good and not for disaster, to give you a future and a hope.*
> — JEREMIAH 29:11 NLT

> *And I am certain that God, who began the good work within you, will continue his work until it is finally finished on the day when Christ Jesus returns.* — PHILIPIANS 1:6 NLT

The One-Way Light (Illuminator)

> *Thy word is a lamp unto my feet, and a light unto my path.*
> — PSALMS 119:105 KJV

Not only does the Word of God reflect light, but the Word of God is light. Wherein the three-edged sword expresses itself as a penetrator and the three-way mirror expresses itself as a reflector or an examiner, the three-way light expresses itself as an illuminator. The Word of God as a mirror reflects your future, but the Word of God as the light directs you to your future. The Word of God as a mirror shows you "what is," but the Word of God as the light shows you "how to." The Light makes the path to your purpose visible and attainable.

Have you ever tried walking in a dark room without any light? Did you stumble or walk into objects? Did it take much longer for you to get to your desired destination? As I think about it, when you walk in darkness you are also fearful because you are not sure if you are going to hurt yourself. Well, the Word of God is the lamp, the candlestick, or the flashlight that you need. It allows you to see your purposed destination and it allows you to see the steps and the path in order for you to successfully arrive at that place of purpose.

The Word of God as the lamp or light only shines one way in regards to direction. It gives you clear direction in regards to moving forward while in your present to your purpose. God's Word always shows you how to go forward. Again, the Word of God as the Mirror shows us the "what," but the Word of God as the Light shows us the "how." The problem for some of us is that we know the what, but we do not know the how. To know what it is that your purpose is but never knowing how to birth it out, or to be extremely gifted with ideas and strategies to better a corporation, enterprise, or any sector of society, but never be given an opportunity is one of the most frustrating situations for an individual to experience. It is like the proverbial rabbit chasing the carrot which, unbeknownst to the rabbit, is manipulated on a string. How cruel is that? Many of you are right there in your life. You know the what, but you don't know the how? You have that business idea stirring in your spirit, you just don't know how to bring it forth. Intuitively, you are convinced that you were created to revive that school system or the educational system as a whole in your city, state, country or maybe even world, but you are overwhelmingly confronted with the question, "How?" You've just obtained that diploma. You've just earned that degree. You've just completed the first step or phase of that project, but now you are asking, "What's next?" The Word of God is that Light. It will direct you to purpose.

Unleash Scripture

Scripture is God's love letter to mankind. It is God's map to purpose. God doesn't want you to be lost. He doesn't desire that you exist in life without having "a clue." The fullness of purpose will not be unleashed until you unleash Scripture. You've had it tied up for some time now and God's Word is just waiting to be unleashed. You have no idea what it is you are missing when you neglect the Word of God. It is full of adventure, history, romance, and wisdom. To be more accurate, I was taught that around 97% of all Scripture falls under at least one of these categories:

1. **Facts to Believe**
2. **Commands to Obey**
3. **Principles to Apply**
4. **Warnings to Heed**
5. **Promises to Receive**

God wants you to believe the facts found in Scripture for your purpose sake. God wants you to obey His commands found in Scripture, not because He has an ego problem, but for your purpose sake. God wants you to apply the principles found in Scripture for your purpose sake. God wants you to heed His warnings found in Scripture for your purpose sake. And God wants you to receive every promise He gave you that is found in Scripture for your purpose sake. God's Word is just for you, but you must unleash it. So go ahead and wipe off that old dusty Bible. Download that Bible app and allow purpose to be unleashed through the unleashing of Scripture. Now is the time! Your purpose is at hand!

Scripture is God's love letter to mankind.

Chapter 4
UNLEASHED THROUGH ANOINTING

I have a question for you. Are you anointed? Think about it and please answer. Are you anointed? If you answered, "Yes," that's great! Now, for my next question. How do you know that you're anointed? Again, please think about it. How do you know that you're anointed? Some of you might have said, "I know I am anointed because I feel it all over me." Some might have said, "I know I am anointed because Pastor Cantaloupe or Bishop Cornflake laid his or her hand on me." Although one might scripturally and rationally argue that one can feel the anointing, you being anointed has very little to do with a feeling. Although one might soundly contend that one receives the anointing by the laying on of hands, the anointing cannot be vouched simply because someone laid hands on another. If you are anointed, and you are if the Holy Spirit resides in you and or on you, but you don't know what it is you are anointed for, then your anointing is irrelevant. Your anointing is inapplicable and becomes trivial when you don't know why you are anointed. Sometimes being able to identify what it is that you are anointed for will be a self-identification if, in fact, you are even anointed.

Your anointing is inapplicable and becomes trivial when you don't know why you are anointed.

The LORD said to Samuel, "How long will you mourn for Saul, since I have rejected him as king over Israel? Fill your horn with oil and be on your way; I am sending you to Jesse of Bethlehem. I have chosen one of his sons to be king." — SAMUEL 16:1 KJV

So he sent for him and had him brought in. He was glowing with health and had a fine appearance and handsome features. Then the LORD said, "Rise and anoint him; this is the one." So Samuel took

the horn of oil and anointed him in the presence of his brothers, and from that day on the Spirit of the LORD came powerfully upon David. Samuel then went to Ramah.

— SAMUEL 16:12-13 KJV

What is the anointing? The anointing is the power of God to do the work of God. It is the empowerment or the enablement to do a God-given assignment. We see in these passages of Scripture, that David isn't simply anointed, but his anointing has meaning. David doesn't simply have a "feeling." David doesn't simply have "hands laid on him" by the great Prophet. But, David and his anointing can both be trusted because he knows what it is that he is anointed for. David is not anointed for anointing sake. David is anointed to be king. There it is! No, David's anointing isn't verified because he feels a warm sensation in his body while he is in the temple. His anointing is validated and actualized because he knows what it is that he is anointed for. God never anoints an individual just because. God always anoints an individual so that he or she is able to do a particular work. "Well, how do I know what I am anointed for?" you might ask. There are three primary ways for you to identify what it is that you are anointed or purposed for.

Ability

God has placed many of the answers to your questions on the inside of you. God reveals purpose through your own natural innate abilities.

God reveals purpose through your own natural innate abilities.

Let's look at our Scripture again.

God has given each of you a gift from his great variety of spiritual gifts. Use them well to serve one another. Do you have the gift of speaking? Then speak as though God himself were speaking through you. Do you have the gift of helping others? Do it with all the strength and energy that God supplies. Then everything you do will bring glory to God through Jesus Christ. All glory and power to him forever and ever. — 1 PETER 4:10-11 NLT

This Scripture makes specific purpose very clear! He says, in essence, if you can speak very well, then that is what it is you are supposed to be doing. If you can sing well, then that is what it is you are supposed to be doing. If you have a special gift for helping others, then your profession will be in a field that specifies in helping people. What it is that you are anointed or purposed to do, you are able to do it well. Isn't that simple! Your purpose isn't to be the head chef at your local restaurant if you cannot cook well. Your purpose isn't to work in the school system or in daycare if you don't like being around, and aren't good with, children. And lastly, but respectfully, you aren't called to sing in the church choir if you can't sing well! It is that simple! Your natural abilities show what it is that you are anointed for.

How would the local church assembly be bettered if we had people in positions and ministries based on this simple yet profound truth? How satisfying and successful would the restaurants that we frequent be if they would hire and position others based on this principle? How highly beneficial would every entity and enterprise in society be if we would just follow this rule? You are purposed to do what it is that you do well! It is that simple! Stop trying to live out someone else's abilities. Stop trying to be a person that you know you are not. The blessing of being you attracts the blessing assigned to you. Being who you are will bless you where you are.

As a child, my grandparents saw my natural musical abilities. They saw me beating on the pots and pans, singing throughout the entirety of the day, and figuring out how to play certain songs on the piano. Realizing my natural abilities, they purchased for me drums, enrolled me in piano class, and positioned me to sing on every platform they thought was feasible for my growth and success. Now the rest is history. My ability showed them my future. In regards to purpose, your natural gifts will give you your spiritual guidance.

The blessing of being you attracts the blessing assigned to you.

Ask at least three people that are closest to you what it is that you do extremely well and have them write them down. It can be a spouse, a family member, a close friend, or even a co-worker. Make sure that they have known you for a substantial amount of time, preferably at least two years. If possible, don't allow them to see what others have said regarding what you do well. We want them to speak honestly without copying what someone else says. Please ask them to write at least three things that you do extremely well. Then write down what you believe you do extremely well. Finally, compare the lists to what others have written and find some of the common denominators. If you asked three people to contribute to this assessment with the addition of yourself and if you have four common denominators, then that is an area in which you are **extremely gifted**. If you have three common denominators, then that is an area in which you are **uniquely gifted**. If you have two common denominators, then that is an area in which you are **potentially gifted**. And if you have one common denominator, then that is an area in which you are **poorly gifted**.

Please be mindful that some might say different things, but are essentially still saying the same thing. For example, one might say that you are easy to talk to or confide in, while someone else might say that you give great advice. They are essentially saying the same thing in different ways. They are saying that you are a gifted counselor. Pay close attention. You may find out that many believe that you are a natural comedian. Some might say that you have a way with children. Or maybe you will discover that many say that you are very creative. This will help to indicate your abilities or your anointing, and your anointing will help to indicate your purpose:

Source #1 (*Please write at least three things you believe that I do extremely well.*)

1. _____
2. _____
3. _____

4. _____

5. _____

Source #2 (*Please write at least three things you believe that I do extremely well.*)

1. _____

2. _____

3. _____

4. _____

5. _____

Source #3 (*Please write at least three things you believe that I do extremely well.*)

1. _____

2. _____

3. _____

4. _____

5. _____

Source/Self #4 (*Write at least three things you believe that you do extremely well.*)

1. _____

2. _____

3. _____

4. _____

5. _____

What are the Common Denominators?

(4) Extremely Gifted in: _____

(3) Uniquely Gifted in: _____

(2) Potentially Gifted in: _____

(1) Poorly Gifted in: _____

After you've taken this assessment, hold close to the areas wherein you were **_extremely gifted_** in and **_uniquely gifted_** in. These areas will help you to identify purpose throughout this book and life.

Passion

Your anointing, calling, or purpose can also be revealed through your passion. Although one's purpose can be revealed through ability, one must marry the ability with the corresponding passion in order to better distinguish purpose.

Let's take the child who is multi-gifted. This child is athletic, has great oratory abilities, can sing well, and play multiple instruments. If this child or the parents of the child are to discern the purpose on this child's life simply based on his or her abilities, this child would never walk in purpose since he or she is multi-gifted. However, although this child is a standout athlete and an amazing spokesman, if you closely examine the child, you will notice that he has a strong passion for music. He participates in sports because he can. He speaks in the classroom and at church because he must. But he sings, writes music and plays the various instruments because he wants to. He has passion or strong desire for music. In regards to purpose, your zeal will reveal God's will.

What is so unfortunate is that so many parents try to live out their unfulfilled aspirations through the lives of their children. Since Father Banana didn't make it to the professional basketball arena, he tries to force Son Banana to be a great athlete in order to go pro, although the son doesn't have passion for sports, but rather has strong passion for music. Or let's take Mother Watermelon. She always wanted to be a nurse, however, she failed in this ambition. Consequently, she grooms Daughter Watermelon to be a nurse all through the child's infant, primary/elementary, and teen years, although this child has strong passion for animals and would probably make an outstanding veterinarian. Regretfully, this child lives an unfulfilled life trying to fulfill the life of her mother. Parents should never use their own passions as a means of leading, raising, and steering their children. However, parents should discern the abilities with the corresponding passions in their children's lives and use the identifying of that passion to "train up a child in the way he should go."

In regards to purpose, your zeal will reveal God's will.

What comes to mind when you hear the term zeal? If I were to tell you, "That young man is very zealous," how would you view the young man without having ever met him? Would you assume that he is unwise or unlearned? Would you presume that he is undisciplined and goes wherever the wind blows? Probably so! However, having zeal or being zealous should not give way to a negative connotation. In fact, zeal is one of the greatest verifications of a leader or an emerging leader. Zeal is evidenced in the child, church member or co-worker who asks the most questions at home, in Bible study or in the staff meeting. Zeal is evidenced in the individual who always has new creative ideas and concepts that he or she believes will better the company, the church, or even the athletic team. Zeal is evidenced in the individual who floods your social media timeline with posts centered around a specific topic such as politics, sports, leadership, fashion, black lives matter, and so forth. This zeal is refreshing! It brings new life to the church, the company, and even the marriage. Enterprises are stale when there aren't any therein who are zealous. The local church assembly is "dead," stagnant, and stiff when there aren't any therein who are zealous. The marriage is without romance, excitement, and adventure when the individuals therein are not zealous.

Zeal is a good thing! However, zeal that isn't properly guided and guarded does more harm than good. Zealous individuals who were not properly and positively guarded and guided resulted in actions and associations such as ISIS, the "Christian" Crusades and other destructive acts. This is why zeal often times gives us a negative impression.

For the zeal *of thine house hath eaten me up; and the reproaches of them that reproached thee are fallen upon me.*

— PSALM 69:9 KJV

And when he was twelve years old, they went up to Jerusalem after the custom of the feast. And when they had fulfilled the days, as they returned, the child Jesus tarried behind in Jerusalem; and Joseph and his mother knew not of it. But they, supposing him to have been in the company, went a day's journey; and they sought him among their kinsfolk and acquaintance. And when they found him not, they turned back again to Jerusalem, seeking him. And it came to pass, that after three days they found him in the temple, sitting in the midst of the doctors, both hearing them, and asking them questions. And all that heard him were astonished at his understanding and answers.

— LUKE 2:42-47 KJV

*And the Jews' Passover was at hand, and Jesus went up to Jerusalem. And found in the temple those that sold oxen and sheep and doves, and the changers of money sitting: And when he had made a scourge of small cords, he drove them all out of the temple, and the sheep, and the oxen; and poured out the changers' money, and overthrew the tables; And said unto them that sold doves, Take these things hence; make not my Father's house an house of merchandise. And his disciples remembered that it was written, **The zeal** of thine house hath eaten me up.*

— JOHN 2:13-17 KJV

In regards to purpose, Jesus the Christ is a prime example that your zeal will reveal God's will. It is so remarkable that when Jesus is 12 years of age, He is found in the temple listening to the teachers, asking them questions and answering questions Himself. What 12-year-old do you know that would stay in the church for at least three days while his family goes home? What 12-year-old sits with the elders of the local assembly for three days wanting to learn from them? At the age of 12, Jesus was showing His zeal and passion for the things of God. The area of His zeal revealed the area of God's will for His life. This young boy who is zealous for learning God's truth would one day be teaching God's truth. Passion is prophecy for purpose! If you find the area of your passion, you will find the area of your purpose.

The sixty-ninth Psalm is considered categorically a Messianic psalm. This means that this psalm is a prophetic psalm concerning Jesus the Christ. If you read this psalm you will discover that many of the Scriptures are prophetically penned concerning the life of Christ. When our writer pens in Psalm 69:9, *"For the zeal of thine house hath eaten me up"* he isn't talking about himself. He is prophetically writing about Jesus Christ. In the Gospel according to John found in the second chapter, Jesus is at the temple in Jerusalem in preparation of Passover. When He arrives at the temple, He discovers individuals buying and selling sheep, oxen and doves. Upon seeing this, Christ gets angry. Christ doesn't have a problem with the marketplace, but Christ does have a problem with individuals turning the temple into the marketplace. With the authority of someone who would have owned the temple, (which essentially He did) Christ chases out those who are buying and selling along with their merchandise like a parent who just came home from vacation discovering a house full of teens, sex, drugs, and loud music. He empties out the money and turns over the tables and says, *"Take these things hence; make not my Father's house a house of merchandise."* Then the Scripture reads, *"And his disciples remembered that it was written, The zeal of thine house hath eaten me up."* Christ had zeal for the temple. Christ had passion for the things of God. This zeal was eating Him up. Here is my question for you. What is it that is eating you up? What is it that you think about day and night? What is it that you often daydream about while in bed? What is it that you have strong desire for?

Passion is prophecy for purpose!

Your passion is a God-given indicator of your purpose. Don't ignore the sound of passion. Don't neglect the cry of zeal. If you neglect your passion, you will reject your purpose.

Using the assessment of your gifts, please list which areas that you were extremely and uniquely gifted in and place them in order in regards to what area you have passion for the most with number one being "most passionate about." Also make a list, if applicable, of areas that you might be passionate about that don't seem to fit with your gifts.

If you neglect your passion, you will reject your purpose.

Extreme and unique gifts that I am most passionate about:

1. _____
2. _____
3. _____
4. _____
5. _____
6. _____

Other areas of passion, *if any:*

1. _____
2. _____
3. _____

Burden

Another way to determine what it is that you are anointed for is by identifying your burden. Your passion and your burden are similar, but they are not identical. Your passion is something that you strongly desire, but your burden is something that strongly desires you. Your passion is something you feel you really want to do. But your burden is something you feel you really need to do. As you must marry the ability with the corresponding passion, you must marry the passion with the corresponding burden.

Again, let's take the example of the multi-gifted child. This child is athletic, has great oratory abilities, can sing well and play multiple instruments. However, this child is passionate about athletics and music. How do we identify what he or she is anointed or called to do? We look for the burden. Although this child practices for countless hours on his jump shot, and although he is passionate about receiving a basketball scholarship, this child is burdened to make a difference in the music industry. He has great musical abilities with the corresponding passion, but every time he sees certain music trends and icons it grieves him. He is deeply bothered by music male icons calling women out of their names. It disturbs him that every music video either highlights sex, drugs, or murder. Although he is passionate about sports and music, he feels deeply burdened to shift culture in the music industry.

Often times, people have asked me the question, "How do you know if you are called to do a particular thing or not?" My answer is an answer that my father in the ministry taught me. You know when you are called to do a particular thing or not because it will be *a burden that you cannot shake*. This is powerful! If you ask a preacher how he or she knew that they were called to preach, many will say that they heard the Holy Spirit. And that I do not question! But I guarantee that if you ask them if it was a burden that they could not shake, they will say "Yes."

Have you ever done something wrong and it deeply disturbed you? You tried to sleep it off and you still felt guilty. You tried to walk it off and you were still troubled. That's the burden you couldn't shake! The same is true when God has anointed you to do a specific work. It will be a **BURDEN YOU CANNOT SHAKE**. We experience it all the time. You are constantly burdened to ask for forgiveness from a person you've wronged. You are constantly burdened to forgive someone who has wronged you. You are constantly burdened to start that business or to quit that job. You are constantly burdened to propose to that young lady. You always try to put it down, but it still has some kind of deeply rooted hold on you and you never feel at peace until you've completely surrendered. It is as if a ton of weights were lifted off of you once you give way to the burden. This is how my mother, who I also mentioned as my grandmother earlier, described it when she finally accepted her call or purpose to preach the gospel of Jesus Christ. Don't neglect the burden you cannot shake.

You know when you are called to do a particular thing or not because it will be a burden that you cannot shake.

For though I preach the gospel, I have nothing to glory of: for necessity is laid upon me; yea, woe is unto me, if I preach not the gospel!
— 1 CORINTHAINS 9:16 KJV

For since I spake, I cried out, I cried violence and spoil; because the word of the LORD was made a reproach unto me, and a derision, daily. Then I said, I will not make mention of him, nor speak any more in his name. But his word was in mine heart as a burning fire shut up in my bones, and I was weary with forbearing, and could not stay.
— JEREMIAH 20:8-9 KJV

We find the Apostle Paul writing a letter to the Church at Corinth. Therein, in the ninth chapter and sixteenth verse, he says that he has nothing to boast about for preaching the Gospel because a necessity or burden was laid upon him to do so. Moreover, he says it would be dangerous for him not to preach the Gospel because God has burdened him to do so. Wow! The burdens that the LORD gives you can be dangerous if you don't correctly respond to it. As Paul said, burden is laid on you, like heavy weights. When you refuse to correctly respond to it, those weights get heavier and heavier all because you refuse to correctly respond to the heaviness of God's call. Could this be the cause of certain illnesses, anxiety, and restlessness?

Let us look at the succeeding Scripture. In this passage of Scripture, we see Jeremiah, the weeping prophet, the one in whom God ordained to be a prophet to the nations, convicted by burden. Jeremiah states that when he prophesied it was always horrible, agonizing news. His prophecies were always about destruction, violence, and death. These messages that God gave him caused him to be mocked, shunned and an enemy to many. Because of this uncomfortable reality and assignment,

Jeremiah thought, or maybe even said to himself, that he wouldn't speak about or on behalf of Yahweh anymore. Certainly we understand brother Jeremiah! There are some things that we stopped doing for the LORD for fear of the repercussion of others. Many of us stopped preaching the whole truth of God. We stopped talking about God's goodness amongst our peers and family. We even stopped living for Him simply because we didn't want others to reject us. However, as Jeremiah is trying not to prophesy on behalf of God, Jeremiah said that this burden to do what it was that God said do was like fire shut up in his bones. He said that it was so burdensome that he could not be still and remain quiet even when he wanted to. It was bothering him from the inside out. I imagine that he couldn't sleep or even eat because of this burden.

Many of you are just like the Prophet Jeremiah. You have been sitting down on your purpose to preach the gospel, your purpose to start the business, your purpose to write that book, your purpose to go back to school, or whatever it may be. But it's just like fire shut up in your bones. You can't continue to sit on your purpose. Aren't you tired of being sick? Aren't you tired of being miserable? You must go and do what it is that the LORD has purposed you to do!

List those top two or three areas in which you were highly gifted in and passionate about. Then out of those areas identify the one or two areas in which you are burdened for. Also list any other burdens you may have, like burdened to help the elderly or burdened to feed the hungry, if applicable. Remember, this is not a passion, but rather a burden you can't shake. For greater clarity, a passion is something you want to do, but a burden maybe something you don't want to do.

Extreme and unique gifts that I am most passionate about and most burdened for:

1. _____
2. _____

Other areas of burden, *if any*:

1. _____
2. _____

Marry Them

Your purpose will indeed be unleashed through your anointing or calling, and your anointing/calling is unleashed through your ability, passion, and burden. The only way to correctly discern your purpose in regards to "*the what,*" "*the when,*" "*the where,*" and even "*the who,*" you must marry the ability with the corresponding passion and burden. Do not be surprised if you discover more than one ability that you are passionate about and burdened for. Whenever this occurs, it is a sign that these specific areas of purpose are to coincide or marry for the sake of your general purpose.

As it is with two individuals who are engaged for marriage, both individuals have their own specific and unique purpose, but the reason why God would call these two distinctively purposed individuals together is because their individual specific purposes are supposed to serve a collective general purpose. These two individuals are stronger and more influential because they are married. All of those gifts and graces that you have, marry them! All of those uniquely different purposes that you discover, marry them. To the pastor, CEO, supervisor or chief authority that has all of the uniquely different personalities, skills, backgrounds and mindsets within those who work under your administration, marry them! It is only when you marry them that the purpose and anointing is revealed on a more powerful and explicit level.

Take some time and marry only those extreme and unique gifts with all of your passions and all of your burdens. If you have and extreme gift for teaching with the corresponding passion, but you have a burden for children in Africa, if you marry those components together, you might discover that your purpose is to teach children in Africa. Maybe you are extremely or uniquely gifted in drawing or gathering a crowd. It seems easy for you to get others to follow you. But also, you have a passion for politics and justice. However, you are burdened to do something in regards to social injustice in your community, state, or country. If you marry those factors together, you might discover that God has purposed you to be a mayor, governor, or maybe even the President of The United States of America. Again, by using only those extreme and unique gifts, marry them with all of your passions and write out a possibility of things that you might be purposed to do or to be. Before you write each one, remember to ask yourself "Will this bless God?" and "Will this bless others?" Please pray and seek God for direction before you write down these possibilities.

Example:

Extreme or Unique Gift + This Passion   +   This Burden   =   This Purpose
Speaking/Teaching   + For people & speaking/teaching+ To lead people to Christ = Preach the Gospel

I believe I may be purposed to: Preach the Gospel of Jesus Christ

Your Turn:

Extreme or Unique Gift + This Passion   +   This Burden   =   This Purpose

I believe I may be purposed to:

Extreme or Unique Gift + This Passion   +   This Burden   =   This Purpose

I believe I may be purposed to:

Extreme or Unique Gift + This Passion   +   This Burden   =   This Purpose

I believe I may be purposed to:

Pray about what it is that you have discovered. Again, purpose is also released through prayer.

Chapter 5
UNLEASHED THROUGH PASTORS

Often times, purpose is unleashed through pastors. This order of impartation was designed by Almighty God. This is one of the reasons why Satan has attacked the pastoral ministry, not just within the local church, but within every sector of society. Please understand that the pastoral ministry is not restricted to the local church assembly or even religious systems. Pastoral ministry types are found in various capacities of our world.

Pastoral Ministry Types:
- Parents (Especially fathers, "The Senior Pastors")
- The President of The United States of America
- Governmental Officials
- Supervisors
- Teachers
- Mentors
- Coaches
- CEO's
- Church Senior Pastors

Each of these operate in a type of pastoral capacity and each one of these pastor types are under attack. Just think about it. Where are the fathers? What happened to the esteeming of the office of President of the United States of America from within and with-out? How many governmental officials can we trust to do the right thing? How challenging is it to find a respectful and respected supervisor? Do the majority of teachers still care about the life advancement of students? Can anyone find or even desire a credible and willing mentor? Let's not even deal with church senior pastors! The pastoral ministry is under attack! However, there is good news. God will always send you a pastor or pastor-type that you need if you obey Him.

Turn, O backsliding children, saith the LORD; for I am married unto you: and I will take you one of a city, and two of a family, and I will bring you to Zion: And I will give you pastors according to mine heart, which shall feed you with knowledge and understanding.
— JEREMIAH 3:14-15 KJV

In this Scripture, God says through the Prophet Jeremiah that He will give His people pastors according to His heart that will feed them what it is they need. We love to quote this verse while omitting the verse that precedes it. God tells His people that if they repent, change their minds and their ways, He will send them godly pastors. Perhaps, the reason why we have ungodly pastors is because collectively we are ungodly people. Often times, the judgement of God is revealed through whom he allows to be the leader. Many times this happens because we didn't treat the godly pastors in a way that pleased God. Just like the old saying goes, "You don't know what you have until it's gone."

And the child Samuel ministered unto the LORD before Eli. And the word of the LORD was precious in those days; there was no open vision. And it came to pass at that time, when Eli was laid down in his place, and his eyes began to wax dim, that he could not see; And ere the lamp of God went out in the temple of the LORD, where the ark of God was, and Samuel was laid down to sleep; That the LORD called Samuel: and he answered, Here am I. And he ran unto Eli, and said, Here am I; for thou calledst me. And he said, I called not; lie down again. And he went and lay down. And the LORD called yet again, Samuel. And Samuel arose and went to Eli, and said, Here am I; for thou didst call me. And he answered, I called not, my son; lie down again. Now Samuel did not yet know the LORD, neither was the word of the LORD yet revealed unto him. And the LORD called Samuel again the third time. And he arose and went to Eli, and said, Here am I; for thou didst call me. And Eli perceived that the LORD had called the child. Therefore Eli said unto Samuel, Go, lie down: and it shall be, if he call thee, that thou shalt say, Speak, LORD; for thy servant heareth. So Samuel went and lay down in his place. And the LORD came, and stood, and called as at other times, Samuel, Samuel. Then Samuel answered, Speak; for thy servant heareth. — 1 SAMUEL 3:1-10 KJV

In this story, we discover how purpose is unleashed to Samuel through his pastor/leader/supervisor Eli. Let's break it down verse by verse.

And the child Samuel ministered unto the LORD before Eli.
— 1 SAMUEL 3:1 KJV

We find in this first verse that Samuel doesn't mind being a student of, and accountable to, Eli. He ministers to the LORD before Eli. This shows that his pastor is watching him, testing him, making sure that he is ministering to the LORD in a correct, beneficial manner. It seems as if Eli is not participating, but rather observing, encouraging, and correcting. Do you hold yourself accountable to your pastor? Do you willfully give your pastor, supervisor, or parent the right to correct you? Do you "know so much" that your leader can't teach you anything? As a matter of fact, do you hold yourself accountable to anyone? Correct posture in relation to your pastor will unleash to you and for you purpose.

And it came to pass at that time, when Eli was laid down in his place, and his eyes began to wax dim, that he could not see; And ere the lamp of God went out in the temple of the LORD, where the ark of God was, and Samuel was laid down to sleep; That the LORD called Samuel: and he answered, Here am I. And he ran unto Eli, and said, Here am I; for thou calledst me. And he said, I called not; lie down again. And he went and lay down.
— 1 SAMUEL 3:2-5 KJV

Please notice that Samuel is positioned so close to Eli that when God speaks to him, he thinks it's his leader. This is a great nugget. Often time, especially initially, when God speaks to you He will sound just like your pastor. Moreover, Samuel's room must have been in close proximity to Eli's room for him to think that Eli called him. My question for you is, how close are you to your leader? When you really value your leader, you stay in close proximity to them. Wherever he or she is, you want to be in that exact place. Successful successors succeeded in seeking the propinquity of their leaders. You must never distance yourself from the one in whom God has called to be your Pastor.

Successful successors succeeded in seeking the propinquity of their leaders.

Also, when Samuel comes to Eli, assuming that it was he who had called him, Samuel said, "Here am I." Samuel was ready to serve his leader. Please remember this. One will never be ready to serve as leader until he is willing to serve his leader. There is something special and powerful in serving leadership. I don't mean being a "tail kisser" or a "brown-noser." But, when you serve leadership out of a genuine, grateful, and sincere heart, purpose and power is unleashed! I can attest to this!

One will never be ready to serve as leader until he is willing to serve his leader.

And the LORD called yet again, Samuel. And Samuel arose and went to Eli, and said, Here am I; for thou didst call me. And he answered, I called not, my son; lie down again. Now Samuel did not yet know the LORD, neither was the word of the LORD yet revealed unto him. And the LORD called Samuel again the third time. And he arose and went to Eli, and said, Here am I; for thou didst call me. And Eli perceived that the LORD had called the child. Therefore Eli said unto Samuel, Go, lie down: and it shall be, if he call thee, that thou shalt say, Speak, LORD; for thy servant heareth. So Samuel went and lay down in his place. And the LORD came, and stood, and called as at other times, Samuel, Samuel. Then Samuel answered, Speak; for thy servant heareth.
— 1 SAMUEL 3:6-10 KJV

We see here a healthy relationship between a primary leader and an emerging leader. Eli, who has aged, discerns that the LORD is trying to get young Samuel's attention. Look at the antithesis. On one end, young Samuel can hear God speak, but, on the other end, old Eli can discern God's voice. Samuel is hearing from God, but he needs Eli to tell him what it is to do with what it is he hears. What a beautiful correlation! Without the teacher, the student couldn't understand that which God was saying. But, without the student, the teacher couldn't hear that which God was saying. Every successful relationship is predicated upon mutual respect and the cognizance of mutual need.

His pastor prepares him for his purpose. He then obeys all of his pastor's instructions and, subsequently, God reveals to him his purpose. This is not the only example of a pastoral relationship found in Scripture. Take a look at these examples:

- Jethro mentored Moses
- Moses pastored the Israelites
- Moses pastored Joshua
- Joshua pastored the Israelites
- Naomi mentored Ruth
- Eli pastored Samuel
- Samuel pastored Saul
- Samuel pastored David
- Nathan mentored David
- David pastored Solomon
- Elijah pastored Elisha
- Mordecai mentored Esther
- Joseph the Carpenter teaches Jesus the Carpenter
- Jesus pastored His 12 Apostles
- The Apostles mentored the Apostle Paul
- The Apostle Paul pastored Titus
- The Apostle Paul pastored Timothy

There are many more pastoral relationship examples found in the Holy Scriptures. God holds the office and role of pastor in high regard.

And if God has high regard for pastors, certainly should we.

When you omit the function of pastor, you omit the fulfillment of purpose. You need a shepherd. The shepherd is the pastor of the pasture. A shepherd secures (protects) you, shows (guides) you, and shapes (feeds) you. Sheep often get lost and in danger. They have a need for a Shepherd. A person who never admits that they too are a sheep will never align themselves with a Shepherd. In the religious system, more so the Christian Church, individuals who "know it all" and are "more anointed and intelligent than others," usually never have pastors. This is because they don't see a need. Even pastors need pastors!

Have you neglected purpose by neglecting the pastors that God has sent your way? Have you allowed your personal preferences to cause you to be distant and distasteful in regards to your supervisors? Have you truly respected and submitted yourself to the teachings of your parents? I pray you have. I pray you will. We need pastors. Through them purpose is unleashed!

When you omit the function of pastor, you omit the fulfillment of purpose.

Chapter 6
THE ASSASSIN OF THE ASSIGNMENT

For we are not fighting against flesh-and-blood enemies, but against
evil rulers and authorities of the unseen world, against mighty powers
in this dark world, and against evil spirits in the heavenly places.
— EPHESIANS 6:12 NLT

Another substitutable word for purpose is "assignment." You were placed on the Earth with an assignment to complete. Yes, you've been given an assignment from the General. It has always been God's intention that you would be a representative of Him within His army. However, just like any other nation's or kingdom's military, God's army has an enemy, the Kingdom of Darkness, which is led and ruled by its General, Satan. Satan was once one of God's right-hand men (angel) until he wanted God's position. One third of God's army thought Satan would make a great General, so they followed him in attempt to over throw God's throne. Needless to say, they didn't succeed. God kicked Satan and those that followed him out of His army. Subsequently, Satan formed his own army and since then up until now the Kingdom of God has been at war against the Kingdom of Darkness.

Satan modeled his army after God's army. It is an organization, which from its origin means that it is organized. The soldiers therein have different ranks and different assignments. Some are assigned to influence different countries, regions, states, and communities. Some are assigned to influence different systems, structures, and sectors like arts & entertainment, media, business, family, government, education and religion. Some are assigned to influence different seats of authority like the seat of the United States President, the seat of governors, the seat of CEO's, the seat of bishops and senior pastors, or any seat of primary leadership. Some are assigned to influence different nationalities and ethnic groups: people of European descent, African-Americans, Asians, Arabs, and so forth. Satan's soldiers have many functions. We call these soldiers evil spirits, demons, devils, fallen angels, and foul spirits, just to name a few. These spirits influence individuals to murder, lie, commit adultery, deny and reject God, be disobedient to parents, and all other unrighteousness. When people intentionally do us harm, we must understand that people are not our enemy. The real enemy is the spirit or the spirits that influence these individuals.

> *But he turned, and said unto Peter, Get thee behind me, Satan: thou art an offence unto me: for thou savourest not the things that be of God, but those that be of men.*   — MATTHEW 16:23 KJV

If you read the context of this text, you will discover that Jesus is getting arrested unlawfully. Peter, His right-hand man, cuts one of the soldier's ear off in attempt to rescue Jesus. Wasn't this noble? Wasn't this a sign of how much Peter loved Christ? Instead, Christ turns to Peter and says, *"Get thee behind me, Satan."* What? Why would Christ say such a thing to His beloved Peter? Isn't he the only one there that is willing to put his life on the line to save Jesus? Why would Christ call Peter Satan?

Christ was not calling Peter Satan. Christ knew that it was God's plan for Him to die for the sins of mankind. The underlining factor was that Peter was being influenced by Satan to put matters into his own hands. Christ looks toward Peter, but He looks at Satan. Let us learn from Christ's example. We must see the face that's behind the face. For every assignment there is an assassin. Evil spirits are assigned to assassinate our assignment. Before you can fully walk in your purpose, you must be aware of the spirits that have been assigned to abort the purpose that is on your life. There are primarily, but not necessarily exclusively, two assassins that are assigned to assassinate your purpose or assignment.

For every assignment there is an assassin.

The Spirit of Fear

According to the National Institute of Mental Health, 6.3 Million Americans have a diagnosed phobia. In clinical psychology, a phobia is a type of anxiety disorder. It is usually defined as "a persistent fear of an object or situation in which the sufferer commits to great lengths in avoiding."

The statistics go on to say, that 30% of the things we fear have happened in the past and cannot be changed. Sixty percent of the things in which we fear will never take place. Thirty-eight percent of the things we fear about our health will never happen. And 90% of the things we fear are considered to be insignificant issues. The National Institute of Mental Health proceeded to name the "Top 10 Phobia's in America."

1. **74%** of Americans are tormented by **Glossophobia**, which is the fear of public speaking.
2. **68%** of Americans are tormented by **Necrophobia**, which is the fear of death.
3. **30.5%** of Americans are tormented by **Arachnophobia**, which is the fear of spiders.
4. **11%** of Americans are tormented by **Achluophobia**, **Scotophobia** or **Myctophobia**, which is the fear of darkness.
5. **10%** of Americans are tormented by **Acrophobia**, which is the fear of heights.
6. **7.9%** of Americans are tormented by **Sociophobia**, which is the fear of people or social situations.
7. **6.5%** of Americans are tormented by **Aerophobia**, which is the fear of flying.
8. **2.5%** of Americans are tormented by **Claustrophobia**, which is the fear of confined spaces.
9. **2.2%** of Americans are tormented by **Agoraphobia**, which is the fear of open spaces.
10. **2%** of Americans are tormented by **Brontophobia**, which is the fear of thunder and lightning.

Fear has a way of clouding your judgement, paralyzing your productivity, and kidnapping your destiny. For many of you, fear has held you hostage to mediocracy. Fear has disabled your creativity. You have not been able to fully live your life for fear of what your family might think. You are too afraid to get a better house, a better job, or even a more fulfilling romantic relationship for fear that you will offend your friends because of your blessings. Many of you never speak up for yourself for fear that people won't view you as a nice individual anymore. Many of you never tell others the truth about themselves or their situations, for fear that you might lose their friendship. And many of you do not walk in your purpose for fear that you will not succeed.

"For the kingdom of heaven is like a man traveling to a far country, who called his own servants and delivered his goods to them. And to one he gave five talents, to another two, and to another one, to each according to his own ability; and immediately he went on a journey. Then he who had received the five talents went and traded with them, and made another five talents. And likewise he who had received two gained two more also. But he who had received one went and dug in the ground, and hid his lord's money. After a long time the lord of those servants came and settled accounts with them.

"So he who had received five talents came and brought five other talents, saying, 'Lord, you delivered to me five talents; look, I have gained five more talents besides them.' His lord said to him, 'Well done, good and faithful servant; you were faithful over a few things, I will make you ruler over many things. Enter into the joy of your lord.' He also who had received two talents came and said, 'Lord, you delivered to me two talents; look, I have gained two more talents besides them.' His lord said to him, 'Well done, good and faithful servant; you have been faithful over a few things, I will make you ruler over many things. Enter into the joy of your lord.'

"Then he who had received the one talent came and said, 'Lord, I knew you to be a hard man, reaping where you have not sown, and gathering where you have not scattered seed. And I was afraid, and went and hid your talent in the ground. Look, there you have what is yours.'

"But his lord answered and said to him, 'You wicked and lazy servant, you knew that I reap where I have not sown, and gather where I have not scattered seed. 27 So you ought to have deposited my money with the bankers, and at my coming I would have received

back my own with interest. Therefore take the talent from him, and give it to him who has ten talents.

For to everyone who has, more will be given, and he will have abundance; but from him who does not have, even what he has will be taken away. And cast the unprofitable servant into the outer darkness. There will be weeping and gnashing of teeth.'
— MATTHEW 25:14-30 KJV

As we revisit this parable in Scripture, we find a servant being strongly influenced by the spirit of fear. Fear is not the prominent factor of the story, but fear is the substratum or the under toning factor of the story. Let us take a closer look at this passage of Scripture and discover the many nuggets in regards to fear.

¹⁵ To one he gave five bags of gold, to another two bags, and to another one bag, each according to his ability.

NUGGET #1

God will never give you something that supersedes your ability to manage it.

This is a powerful nugget! God will never give you something that supersedes your ability to manage it. If God gave you an idea then you are able to manage it. Stop using your weaknesses as an excuse that you are not able. Knowing that God will only give you something that you can manage will help you combat the spirit of fear.

¹⁶ The man who had received five bags of gold went at once and put his money to work and gained five bags more. ¹⁷ So also, the one with two bags of gold gained two more. ¹⁸ But the man who had received one bag went off, dug a hole in the ground and hid his master's money.

²⁵ So I was **afraid** and went out and hid your gold in the ground. See, here is what belongs to you.'

NUGGET #2

The spirit of fear will often follow behind truth.

Have you ever had an idea about a business, a strategy or simply just something you wanted to do, but as soon as you received the good or rather "God" idea, fear came in? God gave you the idea and told you that you were able to do it and then Satan sent to you the spirit of fear. The spirit of fear will often follow behind truth. The Master gives the servant one piece of gold and says you have the ability to increase this and then the spirit of fear tells the servant, "No you can't, so put it away." The reason why fear follows truth is because Satan knows that if you operate in the truth you will bless God, bless others, and bless yourself. Because of this, he sends the spirit of fear in your life so you won't bless God, bless others, and bless yourself. Satan hates you! Perhaps you are still living in poverty, misery, and iniquity because you have allowed the spirit of fear to rule your life.

18 But the man who had received **one bag** went off, dug a hole in the ground and hid his master's money.

NUGGET #3

The servant was too afraid to risk losing the only thing he had.

The servant didn't do that which he was supposed to do with the bag because it was the only bag he had. Some of you God has told to leave your job, but you are too afraid to leave because it is the only job that you have. Some of you are too afraid to leave friends that are unhealthy for you because they are the only friends that you have. Some of you are too afraid to leave that ungodly man or woman because they are the only man or woman that you have. Some of you are too afraid to leave that religious institution simply because it is the only religious institution you've been affiliated with. You never grow and it never grows because you are too afraid to risk losing it. But the perplexity is this; if you don't risk losing, you also do not risk gaining.

> [18] But the man who had received one bag **went off,** dug a hole in the ground and hid his master's money.

NUGGET #4

The spirit of fear will cause you to go into hiding.

The spirit of fear will cause you to go far off into hiding. This servant went away from everyone else for fear of others seeing the truth. Many of you stay isolated from people because of the spirit of fear. You go into hiding. You are afraid that people will discover the truth about you. You are afraid that people will discover that you are flawed, emotional, and sensitive. You are afraid that people will discover the truth about you and then take advantage of you.

But what is so ironic is that you hate being lonely, but you still stay in hiding. Often times, you hear God telling you to call or text that person who you want to get closer to and then the spirit of fear says, "Don't you do it." God tells you to go fellowship and socialize with others, but then fear says, "Don't you do it." Spouses, God will tell you to tell your spouse how they hurt your feelings, but because you fear being vulnerable, rejected or perceived as weak or needy, the spirit of fear tells you to "Stay quiet, stay cold, and stay isolated from your spouse." If you keep allowing the spirit of fear to take you into hiding you will never be fully blessed. You will never walk in your purpose.

²⁴ "Then the man who had received one bag of gold came. 'Master,' he said, 'I knew that you are a hard man, harvesting where you have not sown and gathering where you have not scattered seed.

NUGGET #5

The spirit of fear will always give you false perception.

This servant had a false perception of his Master. He said that his Master was a hard man. But his Master wasn't hard, He was just. He gave everyone duties according to their own abilities. How was He hard? The spirit of fear will cause you to perceive people and realities falsely. Because you've experienced a few relationships with men who were not faithful to you, because of the spirit of fear you now perceive that every man that speaks to you is a "dog". You perceive that your spouse doesn't love you simply because they hurt your feelings. This is due partially to the spirit of fear. You have a new supervisor on your job who does things a little differently and now you do not like him or her all because you fear change. Since your previous pastor was money hungry, a whore-monger, and manipulative, you perceive every male Pastor as money hungry, whore-mongers, and manipulative. This has all occurred because of the spirit of fear. Fear always gives you a false perception. One of the acronyms that you might have heard for fear is "**f**alse **e**vidence **a**ppearing **r**eal." This is one of the reasons why it is so important to walk by faith and not by sight, because often times the enemy will manipulate what it is that you see.

²⁵ So I was afraid and went out and hid your gold in the ground. See, here is what belongs to you.'

²⁶ "His master replied, 'You wicked, lazy servant! So you knew that I harvest where I have not sown and gather where I have not scattered seed? ²⁷ Well then, you should have put my money on deposit with the bankers, so that when I returned I would have received it back with interest.

NUGGET #6

The spirit of fear will cause you to funeralize your gift.

Watch this! The servant buries the gift that his Master gave to him, symbolizing that to him it was dead. It symbolized that what it was the Master gave him had no potential. Listen, God never gives you anything to bury. God always gives you something to resurrect. He gives you a job so that you can resurrect that job in some capacity. He gives you a spouse so that the two of you will resurrect each other in some way. He gives you talents and ideas for you to resurrect. He gives you a local church, not just for you, but so you can resurrect that church in some aspect. He gives you pastors after His own heart, not just so the pastor will bless you, but so you can resurrect that pastor in some way.

You should be sick and tired of burying what it is that God gave you because of the spirit of fear. I speak prophetically that as you walk by faith you are going to resurrect what it is that God has given you. The world needs to know that you're anointed. The world needs to know that you are the head and not the tail. The world needs to know that you are the lender and not the borrower. The world needs to know that you are intelligent. The world needs to know that you are a mighty reformer. You may be asking the question, "Why does the world need to know me?" The world needs to know you child of God, because the world can't know God and until the world knows you. Again, you are His representative on the Earth.

> *For God hath not given us the spirit of fear; but of power, and of love, and of a sound mind.* — 2 TIMOTHY 1:17 KJV

> *A psalm of David. The LORD is my light and my salvation--so why should I be afraid? The LORD is my fortress, protecting me from danger, so why should I tremble?* — PSALM 27:1 NLT

The Spirit of Laziness

26 "His master replied, 'You wicked, *lazy* servant! So you knew that I harvest where I have not sown and gather where I have not scattered seed? 27 Well then, you should have put my money on deposit with the bankers, so that when I returned I would have received it back with interest.

Although the spirit of fear is an assassin of the assignment, the spirit of laziness is as well. With great paradox and parallel, the spirit of laziness causes slow success and fast failure. The spirit of laziness influences you to stay in bed, procrastinate, and do just enough to get by. Yes, mediocrity is most often due to the spirit of laziness. Many entities and institutions are stagnant because people are lazy. We never come up with any new, refreshing ideas because we are too lazy to think of any. How sad! The ideas and concepts that we do have, we are too lazy to execute them. Mediocre ministries, mediocre hired work, and mediocre public services are all due to the spirit of laziness. Some might say, "That is not the case all the time. Maybe some are just mediocre because of the lack of competence." That may be true, but most are too lazy to even go and grow more competently.

With great paradox and parallel, the spirit of laziness causes slow success and fast failure.

Many of us have suffered from this wicked spirit. Laziness will either slow success or stifle success. The Master told this servant that he was lazy. Yes he was fearful, but he was lazier than he was fearful. The Master proves this by saying in essence, "If you were that fearful to lose what it was that I gave you, you could have at least put it in the bank where it would have been safe and it would have gained some interest on it. But you were too lazy to even go to the bank."

Watch this! How is it that he was too lazy to go put the talent in the bank, but yet he wasn't too lazy to go put the talent in the ground? That spirit of laziness robbed him of a lucrative idea. The same energy he wasted putting the talent in the ground was the exact same energy he could have invested putting it in the bank, but he was too lazy to even think. The same energy that we waste posting commentary on social media could be the same energy used to invest in writing a book. The same energy used at looking for a job could be the same energy that we invest in starting a business. Our problem is that we are too lazy to even think of these ideas. Don't allow a lazy spirit to rob you of a lucrative idea!

The spirit of laziness wants you to put off that project or assignment for the next day. And then the next day becomes the next day, and the next day becomes the next day, and so forth. The fruit of poverty follows the spirit of laziness. Although the government might be flawed and possibly corrupt, the government is not your issue. Although people may not be generous to you, unkind people are not your problem. Although you have a dark past, your dark past is not your problem. Your present problem is that you are lazy. If you say that you love God but you are lazy, you are lying. It is impossible to be lazy and loyal! If you will kick out this spirit, you will walk in your purpose.

Lazy people are soon poor; hard workers get rich.
— PROVERBS 10:4 NLT

Despite their desires, the lazy will come to ruin, for their hands refuse to work.
— PROVERBS 21:25 NLT

Chapter 7
GO TO WORK

Acccoording to a 2014 report by the Conference Board, which is a New York-based nonprofit research group, 52.3% of Americans are unfulfilled with their jobs. The survey goes on to prove that what it is that makes employees the happiest while on their jobs is interest in the work.

In 2015, Tony Schwartz and Christine Porath, contributors of Forbes Magazine, conducted a study in partnership with Harvard Business Review to examine the underlining factors of worker engagement. The study identified four important contributors to job fulfillment. The survey indicated that the most important need for employment satisfaction was purpose. The survey furthermore elaborated that employees need to feel spiritually connected to a higher calling of purpose while employed at their places of employment. This survey expressed that individuals who have a sense of purpose while on their jobs were more than three times more likely to stay with that place of employment.

May I submit that many of you are unhappy because you have been operating on a job, but have not yet operated in your work. There is a difference between having a job and having a work. Having a job says that you've been employed by man. But having a work means that you've been employed by God. A job pays you money, but a work pays you fulfilment. A job confines you, but a work liberates you.

It is worth noting that nowhere in Scripture does God command mankind to get a job, but almost everywhere in Scripture God commands man to go to work. Many of you may have jobs in the educational system when in fact your work is on the mission field. Many of you may have jobs in public services when in fact your work is in the health field. Many of you may have a job in banking, but your work is in fashion. Satan wants to tie you down to a job so that you won't be unleashed to do your work.

God never intended for you to work more for a company than you do for Him. For some of you, you have been devalued at your place of employment for too long. You've been overworked, but yet underpaid. Your job doesn't want your ideas. Your job doesn't value your experiences. Your job doesn't appreciate your authenticity. The only thing your job wants you to do is to clock in and clock out. Once you realize your work, you will then realize your worth.

The place of your employment should be a place you work at and not a place you work for. If your God given work is to radically change the culture in the food industry, then you don't work for the restaurant, you just work in the restaurant. If your God-given work is to change children's lives educationally and personally, then you don't work for the school, you just work at the school.

Please hear me correctly. I am not telling anyone to quit their job. What I am telling you is that you don't need a job that's not helping you accomplish your work. Some of you don't have a job and you've allowed that excuse to keep you lazy. However, just because you are jobless doesn't mean you have to be workless. Many of you might have retired from a job, but you don't have to be retired from work.

A job doesn't create work. It's your work that creates a job. Think about it! The shoe company essentially didn't create the work of providing shoes. It was the work of someone seeing the need for shoes and then creating the shoes, that created the shoe company. The soul-food restaurant didn't create the work of providing food. It was the work of "Big Mama" seeing the need of providing food for her family, her church, and then her community, that subsequently created the soul-food restaurant. Essentially, a job does not provide for you work and money, but a work is that which provides for you a job and money. If you change your thinking you will change your living! Don't go to a job. Go to a work!

The place of your employment should be a place you work at and not a place you work for.

---

*And the LORD God took the man, and put him into the Garden
of Eden to **dress** it and to keep it.*   — GENESIS 2:15 KJV

The word "*dress*" in the Hebrew is `abad. It literally means "to work."
Not only does it mean to work, but in many contexts of Scripture `abad
also means "to serve or to worship." Why is this significant? This is
significant because your work is indeed your worship! When you do what
it is that God has placed you on the Earth to do, you are worshiping
God. If you are not at work, you are not in worship! It is much bigger
than coming to the local church assembly with a mouth opened and
hands stretched. Our worship to God is a livelihood of work. Not just
any work, but the work He has called us to do individually. Like Adam,
God gives each of us a garden to dress (work). Please understand that
God assigned Adam to the Garden of Eden, not the "Garden of Egypt."
Are you working the right work at the right garden? Are you working the
"Garden of Medicine" when you should be working the "Garden of
Entertainment?" Are you working the "Garden of Law" when you
should be working the "Garden of Politics?" In more ways than one,
you should never do another man's work in another man's garden.

If you are not at work, you are not in worship!

Many of you young adults who are in your 20's, and some of you who
are in your 30's, have been experiencing what psychologists have coined,
quarter mid-life crisis. You are feeling lost, scared, lonely, or confused as a
result of either not doing your God-given work or because you have not
yet discovered your God-given work. You have become stressed because
you are still single, unemployed, or still don't even know your career
path. You feel like you are going to breakdown because you are not at
the place of purpose. I dealt with quarter mid-life crisis minutely when I
reached the age of 25. I knew instinctively that God desired much more
from me, and for me, than that which was being displayed in my life at
that time. I became depressed and even a bit angry. However, I didn't
just look at my circumstances and complain. I made some challenging

decisions by faith and God blessed me accordingly.

National statistics say that at least 50% of students who enter college are undecided about their majors. This is due to them not yet knowing their work. The statistics express that 70% of students change their major at least once, but most will change their major at least three times before they graduate. This is due to them not yet knowing their God given work. Statistics also share that more than 50% of college graduates pursue careers that are not even related to their majors. This is due to them being unsure of their work or purpose.

1) **Why should I work?**
   a) God worked
      Genesis 2:2; John 5:17
   b) Jesus worked
      John 4:34; John 5:17
   c) The Holy Spirit works
      John 16:7,8; John 16:13
   d) You are commanded to work
      1 Corinthians 15:58; 2 Timothy 4:5
   e) You are blessed when you work
      James 1:25; Revelation 22:12

2) **Why should I have a skill, trade, or place of employment?**
   a) To be an example
      1 Thessalonians 4:11,12; 2 Thessalonians 3:6-13
   b) To provide for your family
      1 Timothy 5:8
   c) To support the work/ministry/calling/assignment
      2 Thessalonians 3:6;13 Paul made tents, The Disciples were fishermen
   d) To prepare for the work/ministry/calling/assignment
      Moses, Ruth
   e) To fulfill the work/ministry/calling/assignment
      Queen Esther, Joseph

3) Why should I leave a place of employment?

    a) If it prevents you from doing the
work/ministry/calling/assignment *Acts 13:2*

Your job should be your ministry and your workplace should be your mission field.

One of the only reasons why God would tell you to leave your job is in order for you to go to work.

"Didn't Jesus have a job that had nothing to do with His God-given work?" you might ask. No, He didn't! His job as a carpenter/builder had everything to do with His purpose. His profession was preparation for, and a reflection of, His prophetic purpose. He was a builder of buildings, but He would soon be the Builder of the Church.

> *And I say also unto thee, That thou art Peter, and upon this rock I will **build** my church; and the gates of hell shall not prevail against it."*   — MATTHEW 16:8 KJV

> *Jesus answered them, "Destroy this sanctuary, and in three days I will **rebuild** it."*   — JOHN 2:19 ISV

Most of the 12 Disciples were fishermen by profession, but their profession was just preparation for, and a reflection of, their prophetic purpose. They were catching fish, but they would soon be catching people.

> *And he saith unto them, Follow me, and I will make you* **fishers**
> **of men.** — MATTHEW 4:19 KJV

God wants us to go to work, not necessarily get a job. The job of the job isn't to provide for you work, but rather provide for you a workplace. If the job that you are on doesn't support the work that God has given you, then that job is not God's perfect will for your life. God wants to unleash to you purpose, but many of you are going to have to unleash from a particular job.

Now is the time for you to go to work! Nothing or no one can stop you but you. If you want to please God and walk in purpose you must walk by faith and go to work!

Now, *may you be unleashed! May purpose be unleashed! And may the blessings of the LORD be unleashed to you in the Name of Jesus' Christ our LORD, Amen!*

Notes

Chapter 1

1. *Blue Letter Bible*, June 10, 2016,
    https://www.blueletterbible.org/lang/lexicon/lexicon.cfm?Strongs=G2889
    &t=KJV

2. *Blue Letter Bible*, April 20, 2016,
    https://www.blueletterbible.org/lang/lexicon/lexicon.cfm?Strongs=H4976
    &t=KJV

3. *West Virginia Wesleyan College*, April 23, 2016,
    http://www.wvwc.edu/library/wv_authors/td_jakes.html

4. *The Biography.com Website*, "Mark Zuckerberg Biography", June 2, 2016,
    http://www.biography.com/people/mark-zuckerberg-507402#related-
    video-gallery

5. Morgan Whitaker, "Once Homeless, Tyler Perry's now a Hollywood
    success. Here's how", *MSNBC*, September 7, 2013,
    http://www.msnbc.com/msnbc/once-homeless-tyler-perrys-now-
    hollywood

6. Efrem Graham, "Dr. Myles Munroe, Wife Killed in Plane Crash", *CBN
    News*, November 10, 2014,
    http://www1.cbn.com/cbnnews/world/2014/November/Dr-Myles-
    Munroe-Wife-Killed-in-Plane-Crash

Chapter 6

1. *Statistic Brain, National Institute of Mental Health*, "Fear/Phobia Statistics",
    April 27, 2015, http://www.statisticbrain.com/fear-phobia-statistics/

Chapter 7

1. Steve Denning, "How To Be Happy At Work", *Forbes*, June 6, 2014, http://www.forbes.com/sites/stevedenning/2014/06/06/how-to-be-happy-at-work-2/#40e9ff2d3c6a

2. Susan Adams, "Most Americans Are Unhappy At Work", *Forbes*, June 20, 2014, http://www.forbes.com/sites/susanadams/2014/06/20/most-americans-are-unhappy-at-work/#1aad033d5862